Enjoy Your Today

*A 30-Day Devotional/Gratitude Journal to help
you start enjoying life one day at a time.*

Shatiya Figueroa

Scripture taken from *The Message*. Copyright © 1993, 1994, 1995, 1996, 2000, 2001, 2002. Used by permission of NavPress Publishing Group.

Scripture quotations are taken from the Holy Bible, New Living Translation, copyright © 1996, 2004, 2015 by Tyndale House Foundation. Used by permission of Tyndale House Publishers, Inc., Carol Stream, Illinois 60188. All rights reserved.

Scripture quotations marked *KJV* are from the King James Version of the Bible.

Scripture quotations marked (AMP) are taken from the Amplified Bible, Copyright © 1954, 1958, 1962, 1964, 1965, 1987 by the Lockman Foundation. Used by Permission.

Visit the author's website at www.shatiyafigueroa.com

OVERVIEW

Introduction

Hey,

I believe you picked up this book because you are ready to enjoy life. I think that you know there's more for you that you haven't quite seen as of yet. Perhaps, your life is going in a different direction than you expected. You find yourself thinking, "I should be so much further along than I am right now. What is my life becoming?" Maybe you're wandering in a bookstore saying, "God, please encourage me, give me some hope." For all I know, you could be on the couch surfing the internet to give you some sort of motivation to get you moving with enthusiasm about life again. I've been there all before, visited that place of frustration and unfulfilled expectations. Moments like these have been used to bring me in closer to God to hear his whispers of love, encouragement, and affirmation. I learned some profound truths through reading God's word on those foggy dim days. I was challenged to believe, to adjust my thinking, to gain a different perspective, and to apply what I read into my very own life to experience results. And you know what? I believe you will experience the same with the transformative truths locked within this book.

During a wilderness, jobless, transitional, uncomfortable season in my life, (*Did you get all that?*) God gave me this assignment to create a devotional book filled with the same pillars of truth that help me to get exuberant about life. I believe you have a task to do right now as well. God can use your pain and disappointment to play a role to get you actively moving in your purpose today.

One day I woke up in a funk, just not happy with the current affairs of my life. While continuing to read the Bible though, the revelation of "enjoy your today" appeared like a billboard with capital letters and bold font within my mind. It came to me as a command, as a correction from God to say, "Hey, you're not enjoying today. You are always looking to the future, to what's next, that you are consistently overlooking the beauty of the present called today. You are alive, and I am with you, that should be reasons big enough to be joyful because temporary circumstances should not dictate the joy and peace that I've given you." This revelation was an eye-opening moment for me as I began to rip off the scales of ungratefulness and discontentment from my eyes.

The reminder of "enjoy your today" woke me up daily as an alarm clock and as my mind started to align itself with it, I began to see change. Nothing can change outwardly without something first changing inwardly. Often, we want circumstances to change, but it's us that must change in some way. Unknowingly, we may have believed a lie, adopted a wrong way of thinking, developed a negative attitude or narrative to keep us where we are, and those are doing more harm than the actual circumstances. I recall shortly after learning this, receiving a job opportunity, which was huge because I was unemployed for three years at that time, oh excuse me, three and a half years living with my parents at 26. So, was this a coincidence that as I started thinking differently about where I was, I soon arrived at where I wanted to be? Of course not and I don't believe in coincidences.

"Enjoy your today" along with other truths within these pages have removed burdens, eliminated worries, caused me to appreciate the present and helped me to enjoy life while being in the crucibles of the process, the journey. It is a continual daily renewing of the mind with this truth that I only have to do-- one day at a time. You see, it's not about tomorrow, next month, or next year. It is all about today, believing God today, trusting in Jesus today, expecting good news today, developing a new thought today, cultivating a good attitude today, being encouraged today, having a grateful heart today, making progress today and focusing on the good today. And when tomorrow becomes today, choosing to do it all over again.

I needed to share with you the scriptures that picked me up when I wanted to stay in bed with the covers over my head filled with confusion, and wandering thoughts of "God, what is happening in my life right now?" "Do you see me?" "Help me!"

I needed to share truths that God revealed, which nudge me to move forward with expectation because many of us probably don't even expect anything good to happen. We're just going with the flow, letting life happen to us instead of us happening to life and I was over that cycle. Aren't you? It's time to engage with life and be intentional about enjoying it the way God always intended you and me to do so.

The combination of scripture, new thoughts, and practical exercises served as a motivator to birth this book and put me on the road to enjoying life. Thus, because I'm on the way to enjoying life means I haven't arrived yet, but I've surely made miles of progress from where I started. As I allowed these scriptures to change my thinking pattern, the complaining and bitter taste of life begin to fade, which left space for some good new things to shine bright and make a grand entrance.

So, I must keep a firm grip on all the promises that keep me going and all the promises that will be revealed to you soon. It's my most profound prayer that you will be anchored on these promises too, and that frustration, fear, anxiety, doubt, and discontentment will lose its grip on you.

The book is titled *Enjoy Your Today* and not *Enjoy Today* for a reason; the day is yours to seize! This day has been gifted and given to you by God. Now, it's entirely yours to enjoy. You have a significant part to play in the course of your day. It is not the circumstances around you that dictates your level of enjoyment. It's your words, choices, reactions, intentions, thinking, habits, motives, engagement with life, and so on. How many times have you labeled a 24-hour day as bad when it probably was just a bad couple of minutes? Think about it. By calling it a 'bad day', you threw an entire day to the wayside without expecting any good to show up. Today and every day is worthy of good and your participation to enjoy!

The layout of this 30-day devotional/gratitude journal is strategically designed to push you in a place of thanks as you begin to enjoy your day and eventually your life right where you are. Renewing your mind is a life long journey itself, so all wrong ways of thinking will not vanish in 30 days, some will though. I encourage you to read and finish this book, then keep rereading and finishing as often as needed. These revelations never grow old because God and his word never grow old! I regularly turn to these staples of truth to encourage myself in whatever tries to rise against me. Now, I have the privilege to share it with you!

Each morning you open this book, you are greeted with:

- A title
- A biblical scripture
- A brief encouraging message based upon the scripture
- A new thought to help shift your thinking in alignment with God's word
- A morning reflection writing space where you can freely journal with God whatever comes to your mind after reading

Each night you open this book, you are greeted with:

- A nightly gratitude writing space where you can jot down the good highlights of your day because there is always something good happening in your life as you look closer. This practical exercise will train your eyes to look for God and the bright spots while contributing to gratitude filling your heart one day at a time.

So, let's get started!

1.

Start Enjoying Life

God keeps such people so busy enjoying life that they take no time to brood over the past. Ecclesiastes 5:20 (NLT)

I find absolute delight in this scripture, for it is a foundational truth that supports the premise of this book. Many people may not associate God with the enjoyment of life, but as the Creator of life, it is his will that we enjoy it also. According to today's verse, God wants to keep us so entertained in our right now, present-day lives that we have no time to think about unhappy moments in our past. Now the past can be, ten years ago, one year ago, or yesterday.

Wouldn't you like to become a person that God keeps so busy enjoying life? Well, one gem to ensure that is by not thinking about the past because it robs us from today. **We give too much energy thinking about something disappointing in our yesterdays, that we stop embracing what God wants to do in our lives, through our lives, right now.** Our best days are not behind us, no matter how successful they appeared nor do we need to mourn the past with regret.

Today, when an unhappy moment tries to revisit your mind, open your mouth, and say, "God is working all things in my favor. Today is a new day, filled with new opportunities and better moments. He keeps me so busy enjoying life that I have no time to think about the past and I choose to enjoy today." I believe as you choose to enjoy one day at a time, you will be enjoying life and the past has to stay where it's at, in the past!

Today's New Thought: God keeps me so busy enjoying life that I have no time to think about the past!

Morning Reflection

_____

_____

_____

_____

_____

_____

_____

_____

_____

_____

_____

_____

_____

_____

_____

_____

Nightly Gratitude

_____

_____

_____

_____

_____

_____

_____

_____

_____

_____

_____

_____

_____

_____

_____

_____

2.

The God Of Today

*Give your entire attention to what God is doing right now, and
don't get worked up about what may or may not happen
tomorrow. God will help you deal with whatever hard things
come up when the time comes. Matthew 6:34 (MSG)*

Well if yesterday's devotional scripture was the premise of this
book, it couldn't have happened without this verse too. Reread
the above verse! These words sound like an order, a command,
and not a suggestion by our Father. It's like his voice projects to
say, **"My child, give your attention to what I am doing today
and do not get caught up in the 'what if's' and the
hypotheticals of life, trust me to supply, provide, sustain for
you today."**

It is apparent that God does not want us to worry about
tomorrow. He wants us to acknowledge him as the God of our
today, and when tomorrow becomes today, to do it all over
again. So often we can give our attention to future due dates, that
we neglect the value of today by being consumed with the details
about tomorrow. At times, we didn't notice the provision for this
day, the wisdom we had to solve a problem at work or that today
the assignment has been completed, because while we're in our
today, we are filled with anxiety for what may or may not
happen tomorrow. God is urging us not to worry and to believe
that he is our helper.

Today, God does not want you to worry about the business
proposal that you must present next week, the bill that is due in
three days, or the job interview tomorrow. He wants you, yes
you, to give your attention to Him starting now without any
worries about tomorrow. Can you do that today?

Today's New Thought: I focus on the God of my today with no worries about tomorrow!

Morning Reflection

_____

_____

_____

_____

_____

_____

_____

_____

_____

_____

_____

_____

_____

_____

_____

Nightly Gratitude

_____

_____

_____

_____

_____

_____

_____

_____

_____

_____

_____

_____

_____

_____

_____

3.

Becoming A Responder

...God does not respond to what we do; we respond to what God does. We've finally figured it out. Our lives get in step with God and all others by letting him set the pace, not by proudly or anxiously trying to run the parade. Romans 3:28 (MSG)

When Paul said, he finally figured it out in this verse; I felt like I did too. When I came across this scripture one morning, it gave me a 'Selah' moment in which I had to pause and adjust my thinking when it came to my relationship with God. "In what way?" You may ask. Well, I heard many sermons on doing, doing, doing, and that always made me feel that if I haven't received a result, a promise that I wanted yet, then I'm not doing enough, so I have to do some more. That way of thinking is exhausting, leads to burn out, brings thoughts of failure, and resulted in not enjoying life. However, this scripture informed and corrected me to know that more than being a doer, I am called to be a responder to God's grace.

Many people are just doing things and not exactly things that God even wants them to do. By being a responder, that means that God has already done something and I'm merely responding to it. Embracing this took away the pressure of trying to make something happen in my life and truly allowed God to be God in my life.

You see, **God sets the pace, he initiates a move, always takes the first step in this relationship with us**, and now we are responding to his instruction, a door he opened, an opportunity he presented, etc... **Our lives consist of responses to God; that's all.** I needed this truth to be at the beginning of the book before you move any further in adjusting your thinking. I hope you see why. This truth is significant to enjoying life and understanding our role with God. Furthermore, the way we view God affects how we receive from him. Now we can see him as the loving God who pursued us, chose us, and continues to make the first move for us.

Today's New Thought: I am a responder to God's grace!

Morning Reflection

_____

_____

_____

_____

_____

_____

_____

_____

_____

_____

_____

_____

_____

_____

_____

_____

_____

_____

_____

_____

_____

_____

_____

_____

_____

_____

_____

_____

_____

_____

_____

_____

_____

_____

_____

Nightly Gratitude

_____

_____

_____

_____

_____

_____

_____

_____

_____

_____

_____

_____

_____

_____

_____

4.

Your Destiny Is Decided

Everything has already been decided. It was known long ago what each person would be. So, there's no use arguing with God about your destiny. Ecclesiastes 6:10 (NLT)

Pretty straightforward verse, huh? Everything is already finished because of Jesus finished works at the cross, including your destiny. God knew long ago, what we were individually called to be and do.

Let's say, God has already decided for you to be a teacher, an engineer, or a pastor. He made that decision about you before you used that gift for the first time or even knew you had it. God wants you to choose what he has already decided. So finding out what you were created to do is pivotal to you enjoying life. A unique gift was deposited on the inside of you the day you were born to demonstrate who God is upon this earth. You may have recognized it or barely used it but know that discovering and developing your gift will help you enjoy the gift of life.

To exist and not know why will contribute to you experiencing frustration in your life or even blaming others for your shortcomings. It can feel as if you are wandering through life instead of having engagement with life. Most people think that way, so you're not alone. Today, talk with God about your gifts. Ask him to show you what you were purposed to do. If you know your gifts, then ask God to help you stir them up in the way he intended for you to use it. Sometimes you can know the gift but misuse it. **I want you to know that you were created for greatness. No matter who told you otherwise, no matter what unkind words you have spoken over yourself or what life has appeared to be as you have known it thus far.** God created you to have a good and full life, start talking with your Creator, whether it's your first time or the first time in a long time.

Today's New Thought: God created me for destiny!

Morning Reflection

_____

_____

_____

_____

_____

_____

_____

_____

_____

_____

_____

_____

_____

_____

Nightly Gratitude

_____

_____

_____

_____

_____

_____

_____

_____

_____

_____

_____

_____

_____

_____

_____

_____

5.

Knowing God's Character

People who don't know God and the way he works fuss over these things, but you know both God and how he works. Steep your life in God-reality, God-initiative, God-provisions. Don't worry about missing out. You'll find all your everyday human concerns will be met.
Matthew 6:32-33 (MSG)

So, let's digest this! "Things" in the above verse is referring to what we may eat, wear, drink-- our basic needs. You can see this illustrated in the scripture before the above verse in the Bible. Jesus is teaching us that people who fuss or worry about these things do not know the character of God while at the same time, looks directly at believers and say but you know God, and how he works, so you should not worry.

Doesn't that statement make you ponder? If you being a believer, say you know God, and how he works, then you will not worry about life. However, if you are a believer and filled with worry, you are acting as if you do not know your Heavenly Father. **There's a dividing line, either you will worry, or you will believe.** God wants you to shift your focus to him and not these things. Then, you will not fear but be empowered to believe.

Today, when a situation rears its head to worry, let it trigger you to think on God, his character, and his goodness. Let it trigger you to give the care to God, knowing that he cares for you *(1Peter 5:7)*. When you do this consistently starting with today, you will find out that the problem is solved and the need is met.

Today's New Thought: I know God and how he works. I will not worry. All is well!

Morning Reflection

_____

_____

_____

_____

_____

_____

_____

_____

_____

_____

_____

_____

_____

_____

_____

_____

Nightly Gratitude

6.

Believe Anyway

When everything was hopeless, Abraham believed anyway,
deciding to live not on the basis of what he saw he couldn't do
but on what God said he would do. Romans 4:18 (MSG)

Does everything seem hopeless in your life right now? Then you're in a great position to believe anyway just like Abraham! Abraham only had God's word that he would become a father of many nations, nothing else just God's word. He believed, and it happened to prove that bold belief in God's word is enough. God doesn't want you to believe just when things are shining bright; anyone can do that. He wants you to have faith when it appears as if the light has been snuffed out. Is it challenging? Of course, but it's possible.

Notice that, before Abraham believed, he first made a decision; a decision in how he was going to live. Abraham decided to live not based on his impotence or weakness but in simply what God said to him. He set a standard for his life; God's word was that standard. Abraham didn't look to himself to make things happen because it was absolutely nothing he could do. His living was based upon his believing, to believe regardless of what he saw or even felt and allow God's word to reign. In like manner, a decision must be made by you. How will you live? Will you believe anyway?

We are called to a higher standard of living, in fact, a higher standard of believing.

When there's no reason to have hope, we still find it because Jesus is our hope! Hope is a person. Yes, this is happening, and that is happening, but when we decide to believe anyway, we choose to live!

Today's New Thought: I decided to believe anyway!

Morning Reflection

_____

_____

_____

_____

_____

_____

_____

_____

_____

_____

_____

_____

_____

_____

_____

_____

Nightly Gratitude

_____

_____

_____

_____

_____

_____

_____

_____

_____

_____

_____

_____

_____

_____

_____

_____

7.

Give Thanks

In every situation [no matter what the circumstances] be thankful and continually give thanks to God; for this is the will of God for you in Christ Jesus. 1 Thessalonians 5:18 (AMP)

In writing this book, I noticed a reoccurring theme, perhaps you will see it too, and that would be "no matter what." As if God wants us to catch the message--- no matter what season, no matter what circumstance, no matter what trial, no matter what difficulty, no matter how much time has passed, you can enjoy, you can triumph, you can give thanks.

So many scriptures talk about being thankful and giving thanks. As you observed in today's verse, we are to be thankful IN every situation, not FOR every situation. Of course, we aren't to thank God for horrible things that happen, but we can still give him thanks in the midst of it all. Even in moments of disappointment and unfair treatment, I gave God thanks choosing to believe that somehow, someway, what happened would work out to my advantage. Romans 8:28 says, "And we know that God causes everything to work together for the good of those who love God and are called according to his purpose for them."

For there is always something to thank God for, that's why every night of this book, you have a writing space to journal and highlight the good. I remember the day I was wrongfully fired while pregnant; I went home and discussed my feelings with my husband. After I let it all out, he asked what we normally would ask each other at the end of our days, "So what was the highlight of your day? What is something good that happened?" As I laugh now, I think my answer was, "I got off early." **Being able to see the good is a disciplined skill, and having a grateful heart creates an invitation for more good to come.** I like to say,

"Find the good and you'll find God." This approach to living, this attitude of gratitude, will bring light into your days.

Today's New Thought: No matter what, I will give thanks!

Morning Reflection

finding the good in needing 20k + allowing Dad to show up for me. Asking for help for the first time ever!!

Jason drinking and the baby situation. Trying to see the God.

Gratitude
- Texas!! - Easy flight - Dad getting safe nm
- Candy & Pascal - supportive Jason
- looking beautiful today for the wedding - watching Aunt Laurel get married.

Nightly Gratitude

8.

Your Words, Your World

The mouths of fools are their ruin; they trap themselves with their lips. Proverbs 18:7 (NLT)

There is a connection between what you speak and what you see. Do you know that not every bad thing that happens in your life is the enemy or another person? Some things happened because you said that it would, your very own words trapped you. Great revelation, right? Another biblical verse says, "Death and life are in the power of the tongue: and they that love it shall eat the fruit thereof." *(Proverbs 18:21) There* is power, creative power within our mouths, and we will harvest the fruit of our words, good or bad.

Do you often speak that nothing works out for you, then nothing ends up working for you? Do you say, "That's impossible to do!" Then you never accomplished that goal? Have you ever said, "No one supports me!" or "I don't have enough?" You see, your words are creating your world. It's time to be disciplined with your speech. **It's time to have your mouth work for you rather than against you.** It's time to speak what you want to see in your day! How much would your day, your month, your year, your life would change if you changed your words? I think exponentially!

Today, be intentional with your words. Speak as if what you say, shall happen! Declare that today is a successful day. Declare that something good will happen to you this day. Catch yourself when you're about to speak something negative. It will take consistent awareness in this area but start talking something different to see something different.

Today's New Thought: My words are creating my world!

Morning Reflection

_____

_____

_____

_____

_____

_____

_____

_____

_____

_____

_____

_____

_____

_____

Nightly Gratitude

_____

_____

_____

_____

_____

_____

_____

_____

_____

_____

_____

_____

_____

_____

_____

_____

On a good day, enjoy yourself;

On a bad day, examine your conscience…

Ecclesiastes 7:14 (MSG)

9.

Think Good Thoughts

*Finally, brethren, whatsoever things are true, whatsoever things
are honest, whatsoever things are just, whatsoever things are
pure, whatsoever things are lovely, whatsoever things are of
good report; if there be any virtue, and if there be any praise,
think on these things.*
Philippians 4:8 (KJV)

Think about good things, good outcomes, good news! Why is it
that five great things can happen throughout the day, but one bad
thing seems to capture our attention? Maybe it was a rude
comment, a dismissive look, an argument, and we're thinking
about it constantly, replaying the situation in our minds over and
over and getting upset again. We choose what we will think on.

You don't have to believe every thought that comes to your
mind, because every thought isn't true and doesn't reflect God's
love towards you. It's imperative that you get discipline in your
thought life. **You must capture those negative thoughts as
soon as they appear and give them no place to build in your
mind.** I call that my "catch it and trash it" technique. Catch the
negative thought quickly, trash it, and replace it with positive
words, God's word, to speak and think on.

The framework of our thought life connects to how much we
truly are enjoying life. I can look back on times when I was in a
bad mood and realized it was because I was thinking bad
thoughts or pondering a hurtful situation which threw me in a
loop of bad feelings resulting in what I used to consider as a bad
day. Today, take authority over your thoughts and fill your mind
with good things.

Today's New Thought: I center my mind on good things, good
situations, and good outcomes!

Morning Reflection

_____

_____

_____

_____

_____

_____

_____

_____

_____

_____

_____

_____

_____

_____

_____

_____

Nightly Gratitude

_____

_____

_____

_____

_____

_____

_____

_____

_____

_____

_____

_____

_____

_____

_____

10.

Things Are Getting Better And Better

Things will get better and better. Depression days are over. They'll thrive, they'll flourish. Jeremiah 30:21 (MSG)

It can seem as if one bad thing after another is happening and you wonder, "Is it ever going to stop and reverse in the opposite direction?" Well, here's some fantastic news that you can begin to think on—things are getting better and better.

I spoke those words by faith regardless of what I saw or faced. I recall, unexpected expenses, not having enough, and just needing something to lift me. You may be feeling that way too. Then, I came across this verse one day. I paused right where I was, a matter of fact, I was in a coffee shop, and I began to say over and over to myself, "Things are getting better and better. I am thriving and flourishing right now." **Remember, we live by faith not by sight, and we must speak what we want to see in the very face of trials.**

If you are feeling depressed, perhaps you're thinking on too many negative thoughts and observing every circumstance around you. Don't let the cares of this world strangle the word of God from your life. Use your authority, open your mouth, and say, "Depression days are over!" Give God the situation by praying. Guard your heart and remember to keep a firm grip on God's promises to you. Oh, I just remembered Isaiah 61:3 which states that God will give you "… beauty for ashes, the oil of joy for mourning, the garment of praise for the spirit of heaviness…" So, if you're feeling heavy, turn on a good praise song, one that makes you smile and dance with hope. Thus, when the thought of, "Oh, I have to pay this. Oh, how is this going to happen? Oh, something else…" Don't get frustrated, allow it to give you another opportunity to exercise your faith by saying, "Things are getting better and better" because they are!

Today's New Thought: Things are getting better and better for me!

Morning Reflection

_____

_____

_____

_____

_____

_____

_____

_____

_____

_____

_____

_____

Nightly Gratitude

_____

_____

_____

_____

_____

_____

_____

_____

_____

_____

_____

_____

_____

_____

_____

_____

11.

God Cares

*A Message from GOD-of-the-Angel-Armies: I am zealous
for Zion—I care!
I'm angry about Zion—I'm involved! Zechariah 8:2 (MSG)*

"I care. I'm involved!" These are the words that God said in the book of Zechariah that jumped off the page to me one morning, and a smile appeared upon my face instantly. It came to me in the time I needed it as with all the scriptures shared in this book. I'm sure as you hear God saying these words to you at this moment, a smile will appear on your face too! "I CARE. I'M INVOLVED. I CARE. I'M INVOLVED."

Like all the scriptures in this book, it's essential not just to read but to believe because at times, our feelings can tell us that God doesn't care because nothing has changed yet. Situations we find ourselves in can say to us that he isn't involved either. We can feel forgotten and that our matters aren't significant to God. It may appear as if things are happening in the lives around us but not for us, which is so far from the truth. Another scripture pops into my mind in this very moment, "It's impossible to please God apart from faith. And why? Because anyone who wants to approach God must believe both that he exists and that he cares enough to respond to those who seek him." *(Hebrews 11:6)* Did you see that? I'm sure you believe God exists but do you also believe that he cares enough to respond to you when you need him?

God is a God of action. He doesn't just see us in a situation and leave us there. Nope, he sees, he cares, and he intervenes on our behalf. God is not like man. So though, people may see you going through a tough time and not lend a helping hand, God will extend his hand to you. **I believe his hand is going to work** for you right now as you choose to believe that he cares for you.

Today's New Thought: God cares for me and he is involved!

Morning Reflection

_____

_____

_____

_____

_____

_____

_____

_____

_____

_____

_____

_____

_____

_____

Nightly Gratitude

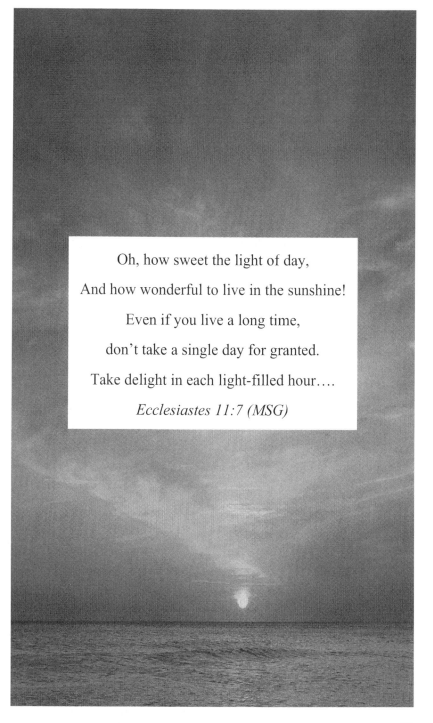

Oh, how sweet the light of day,

And how wonderful to live in the sunshine!

Even if you live a long time,

don't take a single day for granted.

Take delight in each light-filled hour....

Ecclesiastes 11:7 (MSG)

12.

Learn To Be Content

I've learned by now to be quite content whatever my
circumstances. I'm just as happy with little as with
much, with much as with little. I've found the recipe
for being happy...
Philippians 4:11 (MSG)

Paul was speaking in the above verse and discovered an excellent life lesson. He learned how to be content and not be disturbed by circumstances. He acquired the skill in not being uneasy whether things appeared excellent or not at the present moment, and this is what he referred to as the recipe for happiness.

Learning to be content in whatever season we are in is pivotal to enjoying life. **Contentment is not about putting up with unfavorable situations but instead having an attitude that says, "I will make the best of this time as God transitions me to somewhere better."** Isn't it refreshing to notice that Paul states that he learned to be content? For this means, it took some time. He practiced this recipe when trials came his way; it wasn't overnight. Thank God for that! Let's join that contentment class with Paul.

As you have noticed reading this devotional, you are assigned to jot down the highlight of your day. I hope you have been doing this exercise to receive the fullness of this book. The task is to help you to become content right where you are, to open your eyes to see God and the good things he is daily doing in our lives. The more we train our eyes to see good, the more we will experience the good things that God has already planned for us to enjoy, and we just like Paul would be benefiting from partaking in this delicious recipe for being happy.

Today's New Thought: I am content, not easily disturbed by circumstances, and I am happy!

Morning Reflection

_____

_____

_____

_____

_____

_____

_____

_____

_____

_____

_____

_____

_____

_____

_____

_____

Nightly Gratitude

_____

_____

_____

_____

_____

_____

_____

_____

_____

_____

_____

_____

_____

_____

_____

_____

13.

Laziness Is A Thief

The fool sits back and takes it easy; his sloth is slow suicide.
Ecclesiastes 4:5 (MSG)

I know, pretty blunt verse, huh? No grayscale here. We can also replace the word sloth with laziness. So, laziness is slow suicide. When you put it in this context, doesn't that ignite you to start working on the tasks that God has given you?

Each day as we choose to neglect the gifts God has given us, we are causing damage to ourselves. This inactivity is robbing us from enjoying life. God tells us to learn from the ants and be wise in Proverbs 6. Yes, ants! He says no one has to tell the ants when to work. They prepare in one season to reap a harvest in another. He also points us to look and learn from the lazy farmer in Proverbs 24. As you observed his fields in verse 31, it was covered with nettles, thorns, and its fences were broken down. As a result, poverty had become the farmer's houseguest. This illustration shows how a person can irresponsibly ruin what they have and turn something into nothing.

Now, let's look at you! If someone were to walk and observe the field of your life, what would they find? As a musician, would they find clothes piled on top of your keyboard? As a painter, would someone find your brushes broke down, and your easel trying to stand with its two legs? As an author, would they find chapters already completed? Today decide to be a productive person. Do not allow laziness to steal another day from you and know that every step, whether small or big is still progress.

Today's New Thought: I do not permit laziness. My life consists of constant productivity!

Morning Reflection

Nightly Gratitude

_____

_____

_____

_____

_____

_____

_____

_____

_____

_____

_____

_____

_____

_____

14.

Stop Criticizing You

My dear children, let's not just talk about love; let's practice real love. This is the only way we'll know we're living truly, living in God's reality. It's also the way to shut down debilitating self-criticism, even when there is something to it. For God is greater than our worried hearts and knows more about us than we do ourselves. And friends, once that's taken care of and we're no longer accusing or condemning ourselves, we're bold and free before God! 1 John 3:18-21 (MSG)

One evening, I remember saying to myself, "No one is responsible for why you are where you are, no one is to blame, you've procrastinated on ideas, you did this, you did that...." I didn't think anything of the words I said to myself though it left me feeling like a failure. The next morning, I came across today's scripture, and God corrected me with it. I never saw this scripture before, so clearly, I zoomed right passed it because it had always been there in the bible. God told me, "You were too hard on yourself last night." I was astonished by his words because no one would have known I spoke that way to myself the night prior, but God did. He sees all; he cares.

You see, without even knowing it, I was criticizing myself and according to the above verse, self-criticism is not love. Think about that. How we treat others may be obvious to catch, but how do you treat yourself, what words do you unknowingly say to yourself? Think about that.

Don't be so harsh on yourself. You're doing a fantastic job and have made so much progress. And hey, even if you feel you haven't made enough progress in life, encourage yourself to start now but don't beat yourself up with regret. **As condemnation**

and self-criticism cease, more celebratory and enjoyable moments can begin.

Today, I encourage you to demonstrate real love to yourself by speaking good to yourself and celebrating the road you are on with God because it's a good one!

Today's New Thought: God loves me; I love me!

Morning Reflection

_____

_____

_____

_____

_____

_____

_____

_____

_____

_____

_____

_____

_____

Nightly Gratitude

15.
Let God Lead

Anyone who intends to come with me has to let me lead. You're not in the driver's seat---I am. Luke 9:23 (MSG)

In essence, Jesus is saying, anyone who intends to walk with him, do this life with him, has to let him lead, and he must be in the driver seat. For Jesus to even say that he must be in the driver seat is a clear indication that he knows us, humans. We tend to want to drive our own lives. We have a desire to follow our life map and plan instead of following the course he placed in front of us.

You may ask, so what does it mean to let Jesus be in the driver seat? It means that you acknowledge him before making decisions before moving in a specific direction. It means that you ask, "What do you think about me taking this job?" "What do you think about me dating this person?" "What do you think about me moving here or there?" "What do you think of me investing in this?" **It's getting his opinion on the matter and following it.** You see, once God reveals to you the direction, your response, your choice to obey determines whether he is indeed the driver of your life or if you have chosen to take over again.

So, though there are many temptations for you to make decisions without consulting anyone, I suggest you go to God and keep going to him-- one choice, one day at a time, as you commit to making him the driver of your life.

Today's New Thought: God is the driver of my life!

Morning Reflection

Nightly Gratitude

_____

_____

_____

_____

_____

_____

_____

_____

_____

_____

_____

_____

_____

_____

_____

_____

16.
Move, Start, Plant

Farmers who wait for perfect weather never plant. If they watch every cloud, they never harvest. Ecclesiastes 11:4 (NLT)

People who wait for perfect conditions and situations to step out, to make progress, will never move. People who are just waiting to be discovered or for someone to give them an opportunity will remain idle with so much fruit, purpose, and gifting locked within them. Have the attitude of the farmers, "I see the clouds, but I am still planting."

To illustrate this point further, looking at situations around us are designed to keep us stagnant and fruitless, but that's why God instructs us to walk by faith and not by sight. *(2 Corinthians 5:7)* It was never in his plan for us to observe all these outside variable factors to determine whether we would submit to his voice. **God desires that we proceed with the assignment because he has spoken not because we consulted our bank accounts, schedules, or current situations.**

What is the task that God has given you, but your feet never corresponded because you are observing everything else instead of his word? What perfect checklist have you created that you must accomplish before you start? What false scenery do you have in your mind that must happen before you take action? Beloved, God wants you to start even in imperfect conditions. It proves that you are looking unto him. Today is a good day to start!

Today's New Thought: I can start right now, where I am, looking unto Jesus!

Morning Reflection

Nightly Gratitude

_____

_____

_____

_____

_____

_____

_____

_____

_____

_____

_____

_____

_____

_____

_____

_____

No procrastination.

No backwards looks.

You can't put God's kingdom
off till tomorrow.

Seize the day!

Luke 9:62 (MSG)

17.
Step Out Today

When Jesus saw him and knew he had been ill for a long time, he asked him, 'Would you like to get well?' 'I can't sir,' the sick man said, 'for I have no one to put me into the pool when the water bubbles up. Someone else always gets there ahead of me. John 5:6-7 (NLT)

To believe that this man stood in the same condition for 38 years, simply because he was waiting for someone to put him into the pool, astonished me! The good ending to this story was that Jesus came along and healed him. But let's examine this man further, shall we? It wasn't just his idleness that struck me, but the fact that he had been in a position so long that he developed the wrong perspective. He believed that someone should have helped him. Furthermore, he made no progress looking to the help of man.

God wants us to look to him for opportunities, promotion, healing, deliverance, everything, and not people. **Can God use people to bless us? Yes. Should we look to them as our source? No.** We are not to seek people, to "put us on," "put us in," or "hook us up." We are to look unto God. For it is his will, that we make progress, exactly where we are, with the resources we have. "What resources?" you may ask, well time can be one and transferring ideas unto paper can be another. We must make an exploration of what's right in front of us.

Beloved, are you sitting in a place of idleness? Have you been there so long that you developed a wrong perspective? Identify that crazy thought and replace it with the word of God. Are you looking unto people to give you an opportunity? Are you disappointed that the prospect has not arrived yet? Are you ready to make progress with the resources that you have this moment? The decision is yours today!

Today's New Thought: I have everything that pertains to life and godliness. *(2 Peter 1:3)* I am equipped to step out today!

Morning Reflection

_____

_____

_____

_____

_____

_____

_____

_____

_____

_____

_____

_____

_____

Nightly Gratitude

18.

You Are The Equipment

Don't think that you have to put a fund-raising campaign before you start. You don't need a lot of equipment. You are the equipment. Matthew 10:9-10 (MSG)

Get rid of the mindset that you need a whole lot of things before you can begin the ideas that God put within your heart. The truth is you are the equipment, you are the main ingredient that God wants to use, and you can get moving along right now by keeping it simple.

The notion that the project has to be perfection to be released into the world is one that you must erase today. It's a lie that you led yourself to believe, and it's a lie that is keeping you in the same place with no results. You don't want to release the idea because it has to be perfect and that thought is why you have utterly nothing to show for it. No one has ever seen the idea that you have been talking about for months or years. This can be tough to swallow, I know. I have been there, and God had to reveal this to me, so I can start making progress in the things he wanted me to do, like writing this book. Now, I get to share this truth with you, so you can go and make your mark in this world.

You are God's idea, his masterpiece, and he has equipped you with everything you need to win in life. Everything you are searching for is in you and within your reach. Even Jesus used a boat as a pulpit to do what God called him to do. *(Matthew 13:2)* So, improvise!

Today, be empowered to execute ideas and move forward in your purpose because small progress is still progress.

Today's New Thought: God says, I am the equipment; therefore, I am equipped!

Morning Reflection

_____

_____

_____

_____

_____

_____

_____

_____

_____

_____

_____

_____

_____

_____

_____

_____

Nightly Gratitude

_____

_____

_____

_____

_____

_____

_____

_____

_____

_____

_____

_____

_____

_____

_____

_____

19.

The Best Route May Not Be
The Shortest

*When Pharaoh finally let the people go, God did not lead them
along the main road that runs through the Philistine territory,
even though that was the shortest route to the Promised Land.
God said, 'If the people are faced with a battle, they might
change their minds and return to Egypt.' So, God led them in a
roundabout way through the wilderness toward the Red Sea.
Thus, the Israelites left Egypt like an army ready for battle.*
Exodus 13:17-18 (NLT)

God just delivered the children of Israel from being enslaved by
Egypt, and he had a detailed escape route. So exciting, that God's
choice of escape did not include the path that was near or shorter.
Why? For he considered the effects that this trip may bring on
the children of Israel and did not want it to harm them in such a
way, that they would decide to return to the very place he
delivered them from. So, he led them a different, more extended
route to get them to the Promised Land.

Wouldn't you love for God to take the quick route when it comes
to you? **But unbeknownst to your understanding at times, the
shorter distance may seem logical to one's eye, appears
better, but may bring more harm than good and God knows
that!** He foresees what may be too much or too harsh for you
that would tempt you to give up and walk away. So, in protective
daddy mode, God maps out another way. On this route, it is
longer, there's development too, but it won't crush you, for he has
gone ahead of you to guarantee that you will arrive!

Today know that, as much as God wants to get you to your
Promised Land, your destiny, he does not want you to get there

hurt and unprepared. You are his investment, his treasure, and just like the children of Israel, when it's all said and done, you will be equipped and ready!

Today's New Thought: God's route is the best route for me. He loves me!

Morning Reflection

_____

_____

_____

_____

_____

_____

_____

_____

_____

_____

_____

_____

_____

Nightly Gratitude

_____

_____

_____

_____

_____

_____

_____

_____

_____

_____

_____

_____

_____

_____

_____

_____

20.

How Is Not Your Business

Zechariah said to the angel, how can I be sure this will happen?
I'm an old man now, and my wife is also well along in years.
Luke 1:18 (NLT)

This is the very moment where God is showing Zechariah what is to come. God reveals to him many things such as his wife Elizabeth will have a child named John, that he will be filled with the Holy Spirit before his birth, that he will turn many Israelites to The Lord, prepare the way for the coming of Jesus, along with other instructions. Now, after all these marvelous decrees to Zechariah, his response is how.

Now, you can quickly jump on Zechariah and say, "God just told you all these amazing things, and your response wasn't, "Thank you, Lord!" But in like manner, you have been in the same position. God can show you in advance what you will be doing, and your response is how rather than I believe. You automatically think that you have to do something, and even if you do not, you still have the urge to know God's A-Z plan. Often, your first reaction is how, because of doubt, when it should be wow because you believe.

Today, erase the how's and thank God for the wow's. When the question of how comes to mind, use it as a moment to release thanks! Thank God for the visions, dreams, and ideas that he put within your heart. Thank God that they shall surely come to pass because you believed what he said. **Beloved, you do not need to know how for it to come to pass in your life because timing is God's business, and trusting him is yours.**

Today's New Thought: How is not my business, I trust and believe!

Morning Reflection

_____

_____

_____

_____

_____

_____

_____

_____

_____

_____

_____

_____

_____

_____

_____

_____

Nightly Gratitude

_____

_____

_____

_____

_____

_____

_____

_____

_____

_____

_____

_____

_____

_____

_____

21.

It Will Not Be Delayed

This vision is for a future time. It describes the end, and it will be fulfilled. If it seems slow in coming, wait patiently, for it will surely take place. It will not be delayed. Habakkuk 2:3 (NLT)

The above verse is God's reply to the complaining of his prophet. Habakkuk did not like what he was seeing around him. However, God's response calmed all his complaints. God reassured him that the vision is for a future time. So, if it seems slow in coming, wait patiently, for it will take place with no delays!

How comforting are those words of our Father to ease our soul? God gives us hope, confidence, and firmness that the vision shall come to pass. **Not every idea that God gives us is for right now. It plays as a glimpse from Heaven, of what is to be.** Therefore, patience is required. When our minds begin to race, and our eyes are tempted to yield to what we see, our faith must rise and couple with patience.

There may be several things that seem like they are slow in coming for you. Today, you may be expecting a call from an audition you went on or a job you interviewed for because it's been days or even weeks already. You may be expecting that your boss will call you into his/her office to offer you a promotion. You are probably hoping that invitation to come or an acceptance letter to show up because months have passed by without hearing a response. Today, know with full assurance that it will be fulfilled, it will surely take place, and it will not be delayed.

Today's New Thought: Despite what it seems, it will take place with no delays!

Morning Reflection

_____

_____

_____

_____

_____

_____

_____

_____

_____

_____

_____

_____

_____

_____

_____

_____

Nightly Gratitude

22.
Your Character Is Being Tested

Until the time came to fulfill his dreams, The Lord tested Joseph's character. Psalm 105:19 (NLT)

Firstly, I find it astonishing to see details about Joseph's life in the book of Psalm, when the majority is in the book of Genesis. This scripture was placed hundreds of pages later in the Bible as if God wanted us to know something else about Joseph's life. So, here it goes: In between the time in which your dreams were revealed to you, and when you are walking in them, God is developing your character.

For God, it is not just about our dreams being fulfilled but that we have the character to walk in them. He is invested in our growth, that we may show Jesus and be a light to this world while fulfilling our dreams. It is indeed God's dream that we walk in ours successfully with integrity.

Furthermore, when you are tempted to get anxious and desire to be fully positioned in your purpose before its time, know that God will strengthen you from within. As a good father, he does not want you to have anything prematurely. So, God may be helping you to be more patient, to speak gracious words, or to control your anger. For God knows what areas you may be weak in at times, and it is his loving nature that he refines your character so that you can be effective in the calling.

Today's New Thought: God is developing my character for his calling!

Morning Reflection

Nightly Gratitude

23.

Adjust Your Schedule To God's Timing

Now Sarai, Abram's wife, had not been able to bear children for him. But she had an Egyptian servant named Hagar. So, Sarai said to Abram, "The Lord has prevented me from having children. Go and sleep with my servant. Perhaps I can have children through her....
Genesis 16:1-2 (NLT)

Hmm... This statement from Sarai to her husband Abram was false; God was not trying to keep her from having children. He revealed this to Abram earlier in the 15th chapter of Genesis. It was entirely in God's loving plan for Sarai to be fruitful and have children. However, it did not happen on her schedule, so she interpreted not being able to give birth right now, as a "no" from God. She started forming her action plan to help God out and went further and further in the wrong direction.

Sounds familiar? How many times, have you done that? Perhaps, you came up with a timeline of when you should get married, have kids, launch this business, expand it there, and over there too. You have constructed a list in your mind with a due date already attached to it. Furthermore, when that date passes, you are disappointed, frustrated, and make false statements about God. When in fact, you never inquired of God, acknowledged him as being God in this specific matter, or paused to allow him to give you his feedback.

Beloved, God has his set times when things are to happen in your life and not a year, week, or hour sooner. **He is not trying to keep any good thing from happening to you.** God is strategically setting them up to come your way. So, throw your plan away and yield to his.

Today's New Thought: God is not holding any good thing from me. He is making everything beautiful in his timing, just for me! *(Psalm 84:11, Ecclesiastes 3:11)*

Morning Reflection

_____

_____

_____

_____

_____

_____

_____

_____

_____

_____

_____

_____

Nightly Gratitude

_____

_____

_____

_____

_____

_____

_____

_____

_____

_____

_____

_____

_____

_____

_____

_____

24.
Do Not Compare

How do you expect to get anywhere with God when you spend all your time jockeying for position with each other, ranking your rivals and ignoring God? John 5:44 (MSG)

For Jesus to ask this question, it's apparent that people were comparing and competing with one another, just as they still are today. God advises us that participating in comparison gets us nowhere with him and serves as a waste of time. For when we try to keep up with people, we are ignoring God.

God does not want us tangled in the ropes of comparison. He does not want us to look to our right or left to determine what we should have. **When our eyes are on others, we blur our vision from seeing what God is currently doing in our lives.** People who compare themselves amongst others are never satisfied with the victories they receive. They are always looking at others, making them their standard of measurement.

Be honest with yourself today; are you comparing or competing with others? Are you staring at your neighbor's fruit while neglecting to enjoy yours? Comparison is indeed robbing you from enjoying life. Today, walk away from comparison and walk into the impressive garden that God has laid out for you. I am confident that you will begin to enjoy the fruits that grow in your very own garden as you adjust your focus. As a final point, know that the God who shows up for others is the same God that will show up for you!

Today's New Thought: I do not compare myself with others. My focus is on Jesus, enjoying the fruit that he has given me!

Morning Reflection

_____

_____

_____

_____

_____

_____

_____

_____

_____

_____

_____

_____

_____

_____

_____

_____

Nightly Gratitude

_____

_____

_____

_____

_____

_____

_____

_____

_____

_____

_____

_____

_____

_____

_____

_____

25.

You Are An Original

Since this is the kind of life we have chosen, the life of the Spirit, let us make sure that we do not just hold it as an idea in our heads or a sentiment in our hearts, but work out its implications in every detail of our lives. That means we will not compare ourselves with each other as if one of us were better and another worse. We have far more interesting things to do with our lives. Each of us is an original. Galatians 5:25-26 (MSG)

Yesterday, you learned that God does not want us to compare ourselves with each other. To take it a step further, God reveals through Paul that we have far more interesting things to do with our lives. For each of us is an original. I believe the 'far more interesting things' pertains to us as individuals walking in our purpose and discovering what God has called us to do upon this earth.

We have been created directly and personally by God, not to copy or imitate another. We are originals with individual callings and must run our race. When each person takes on the assignment in finding out who they are in Christ and what they were created to do through him, that alone will keep him or her occupied. Additionally, we will have no time to compare ourselves or look at someone else's fruit in their garden because we are actively aware and engaged in what God is doing in our lives.

Let the lie that you are not enough be removed today! **You are enough. You are special. You are an original.** Today, ask God to reveal your uniqueness, that special thing you were created to do that sets you apart from others. Be intentional about spending time with God and getting to know him more, because as you get to know him intimately, you actually will discover your identity.

Today's New Thought: God has made me an original!

Morning Reflection

_____

_____

_____

_____

_____

_____

_____

_____

_____

_____

_____

_____

_____

_____

_____

Nightly Gratitude

26.

Be Free From People

There's trouble ahead when you live only for the approval of others, saying what flatters them, doing what indulges them...
Luke 6:26 (MSG)

Living for the approval of others is dangerous territory, especially in this social media world today. For when we live for the approval of others, we will crumble by their criticism because we held their words so highly in our lives. It is indeed God's word and his words alone that should anchor us or move us into action.

Apostle Paul states in Galatians 1:10, "Obviously I'm not trying to win the approval of people, but of God. If pleasing people were my goal, I would not be Christ's servant." **Our actions and decisions should not rely upon a nod of acceptance from another person but of God.** If our goal is to please people, then we forfeit the privileges of being a servant of God. How? Well, as Christ servant, we must be free from people to be used by God, yielding ourselves to his voice alone. Is it okay to receive advice from others? The word of God tells us to receive godly counsel but remember you asked for advice, not approval.

Beloved, desiring acceptance from others will interrupt your enjoyment of life. You will seesaw each day in your decision-making. You will be uncertain in whom God made you and what he has called you to do. Know with full assurance that you have been approved and accepted by God while you were in your mother's womb. *(Jeremiah 1:5)* So there is no need to take off the garment of God's approval to replace it with an opinion of another. Today ask yourself, "Am I a man pleaser or a God pleaser?" "Do I do things to seek the approval of people or God?" "What is the motivating factor behind my decisions?"

"Do I need people's stamp of approval to feel good about myself and the work I have accomplished?"

Today's New Thought: I am stamped, approved, and validated by God!

Morning Reflection

_____

_____

_____

_____

_____

_____

_____

_____

_____

_____

_____

_____

_____

_____

Nightly Gratitude

_____

_____

_____

_____

_____

_____

_____

_____

_____

_____

_____

_____

_____

_____

_____

27.

Forget The Past And Move On

Forget about what's happened; don't keep going over old history.
Be alert, be present. I'm about to do something brand new. It's
bursting out! Don't you see it? Isaiah 43:18-19 (MSG)

Forget about the past! I know I mention this in day one but it's so worth repeating and while you're doing that---stop rehearsing those hurtful moments too. Instead, be alert, be conscious of what God is doing in your life today. The above verse also states that God is doing something brand new, then is followed up by a profound question, "Do you see it?" I thought, "Why would God asked that question?" Then it dawned on me, could it be possible that we cannot see the new things that God is doing in our lives because we are so focused on the old, the past?"

When we continuously relive these hurtful stories in our past, we are bringing bitterness into our present. We must stop giving voice to the past and talking about it from a victim perspective every chance we get, allowing it to shift us back to that moment as if it had just happened yesterday.

I know that painful situation of betrayal or rejection has hurt you, but you cannot let it paralyze you. You must use the old rumbles of the past to be a motivator to move forward. You can let the former go when you know that God has something remarkable and new in store for you. Holding on to the past with one hand while hoping for the new in the other does not bring you closer to enjoying life. Today, choose to let go of the past and every negative emotion associated with it. Refuse to remain stagnant. Forget the former things and happily move on.

Today's New Thought: I no longer rehearse the pain of the past, but I open myself up to the new that God is doing in my life right now!

Morning Reflection

_____

_____

_____

_____

_____

_____

_____

_____

_____

_____

_____

_____

_____

_____

_____

_____

_____

_____

_____

- ---

Nightly Gratitude

28.

You Will Not Drown

When you go through deep waters, I will be with you. When you go through rivers of difficulty, you will not drown... Isaiah 43:2 (NLT)

We would rather skip over trials or better yet urn in the opposite direction to avoid it altogether. However, we just read that when we go through the deep waters and those rivers of difficulty that life throws our way at times, we will not drown. Doesn't it bring comfort to know that when we go through a hurdle, we have a partner, we are not alone, that God is right there and we will come out on top?

As I read this scripture, I remembered God telling me, **"The reason why you will not drown by the deep waters and rivers of difficulty is that I have called you to walk on top of the water!** How can you drown by anything that I have empowered you to walk on top of?"** This goes for you too this day. Regardless of the situation that you are currently facing whether it is the unimpressive amount in your bank account, the conflict in your relationship, or the long never-ending list of tasks to accomplish your goals --know that it's all subject to change and you will not drown. The storm will not take you under in spite of its strong winds when it simmers down and depart; you will be standing.

Today, speak in the face of adversity and say, "I will not drown; God is with me." You might have to say this seventy times this day but the more you speak it, the more you will believe it and eventually will be reigning and walking on top of the water as God always intended.

Today's New Thought: I will not drown by this deep water because God has caused me to walk on top of it!

Morning Reflection

_____

_____

_____

_____

_____

_____

_____

_____

_____

_____

_____

_____

_____

_____

_____

Nightly Gratitude

_____

_____

_____

_____

_____

_____

_____

_____

_____

_____

_____

_____

_____

_____

_____

_____

29.
God Is Your Personal God

When you're between a rock and a hard place, it won't be a dead end-- Because I am God, your personal God... Isaiah 43:2 (MSG)

When surrounded by pressure from several different angles, maybe finances, relationships, career, health, children, or a combination of these and others, God will personally get you out of those tight spaces. He will personally cause victory to spring forth in your life right amid unfavorable circumstances. He indeed will be your personal God.

Let's say you had a personal shopper whose responsibility is to shop for things that are specific unto you, your style, and interest. In like manner, when the bible states that God is your personal God, he is specifically strategically looking to deliver, to help, to heal, to defend, to protect, to prosper you in every area of your life that needs his help.

I have also learned that at times, **God wants us to grow in uncomfortable places because he is more concerned with our growth than our comfort.** I believe we both can agree that being between a rock and a hard place surely is an uncomfortable place. Thus, I know it could look dark, and you're wondering where is the uphill or the turnaround. Things don't add up, and you are trying to make sense of it all. Please be reassured by today's scripture that with God, you will never reach a dead end. You will not be stuck, stranded, or without options because God is your personal God.

Today's New Thought: There are no dead ends with my God!

Morning Reflection

_____

_____

_____

_____

_____

_____

_____

_____

_____

_____

_____

_____

_____

_____

_____

_____

Nightly Gratitude

_____

_____

_____

_____

_____

_____

_____

_____

_____

_____

_____

_____

_____

_____

_____

_____

30.

Bears Fruit In Every Season

But blessed is the man who trusts me, GOD, the woman who sticks with GOD. They're like trees replanted in Eden, putting down roots near the rivers—Never a worry through the hottest of summers, never dropping a leaf, Serene and calm through droughts, bearing fresh fruit every season. Jeremiah 17:7-8 (MSG)

Through every season of life, you can still bear fruit! I remember when I saw this verse, I had to read it twice! Like, did it just say that? I recall asking, "Am I still capable of bearing fruit during this jobless transitional season?" The answer is YES!!! Though external things may change, you are equipped by God to produce fruit in your life. **You can win in the season you're in because God is with you!** God being for you, gives you the advantage every time.

Trusting God, placing your confidence in him and not in other things or people is the key to bearing fruit in this very season. No matter what season you find yourself in, trust is required for fruit to grow where you are.

According to today's verse, you will be worry free, serene, and calm as you trust and stick with God in this season. I know it may be uncomfortable and new territory, but the same God is with you. So, change your perspective about where you are. Matter of fact, embrace this season because there are good things wrapped up in it. Then expect to bear fresh fruit in your relationships, career, finances, health, in every area of your life because you chose to trust in God's love for you today.

Today's New Thought: I bear fruit in every season!

Morning Reflection

Nightly Gratitude

_____

_____

_____

_____

_____

_____

_____

_____

_____

_____

_____

_____

_____

_____

_____

Made in the USA
Lexington, KY
03 September 2019